D0857119

COWS
ON ICE &
OWLS
IN THE BOG

COWS
ON ICE &
OWLS
IN THE BOG

THE WEIRD AND WONDERFUL WORLD
OF SCANDINAVIAN SAYINGS

Compiled by Katarina Montnémery

Illustrated by Nastia Sleptsova

Hardie Grant

QUADRILLE

Contents

Introduction

The rise in popularity of the Scandinavian aesthetic over the past decade has been nothing short of phenomenal. Our clothes, our furniture, our lifestyles... we've tried *hygge* and *lagom* for our wellbeing, we've IKEA'd every last square inch of our homes. We've lapped up Nordic noir and Danish killings, while scoffing Swedish meatballs. The rest of the world sees Scandinavians as the arbiters of taste, equality and cool elegance. Their politicians and laws are more enlightened, and their style is beyond reproach.

If you've immersed yourself in Scandi-culture, you'll know that there are aspects of the language and sense of humour that separate these territories from the rest of the world. Some might suggest, 'eccentric' sense of humour... where else in the world would the concept of 'shitting in the blue cupboard' make for a common phrase?

It turns out that Scandinavian idioms are both fascinating and funny – often alluding to animals, foodstuffs and climate, in equal measure. As in the English language, creatures like cats and dogs crop up frequently, but who knew owls could be so significant? As you'd expect from these northerly nations, there are plenty of references to the cold weather, the outdoor life and manly beards.

Perhaps we should adopt some of these fabulous expressions into our own language? Who wouldn't love to slide in on a shrimp sandwich or learn where a chicken pees from? Clear as sausage broth? Excellent – enjoy!

Dumber than the train

SWEDISH

Dummare än tåget

While the Brits might call someone 'as daft as a brush', if you want to insult a Swede, compare his intelligence to a train's and then make a sharp exit.

The saying dates from the 19th century, when steam locomotives were commonly named in honour of members of the royal family. One of the first engines to arrive in Sweden, in 1856, was named after young Prince August. It was common knowledge that the prince was not blessed with great intelligence, but as it was treasonous to mock the royals, people would instead make reference to the engine that bore his name. Thus one might insult a fellow citizen by saying that they were 'dumber than the train'.

The death of one person, the bread of another person

DANISH

Den enes død, den andens brød

Or more concisely, 'bread or dead'. The equivalent of the English expression 'one man's loss is another man's gain', this saying originates from the old Viking practice of making bread with tree bark and hay (which isn't quite as appetising as Danish pastries and *smørrebrød*); it certainly doesn't sound as healthy as today's dark, compact, wholegrain bricks known as *rugbrød* (rye bread). Could this Dark Age practice have been the cause of the first fatal case of gluten intolerance?

Own land strawberry; other land blueberry

FINNISH

Oma maa mansikka; muu maa mustikka

Each Nordic country believes that *their* berries are the sweetest in the world, and the short season of their favourite national fruit is as hotly anticipated as an ABBA reunion. For the Finn, no berry is superior to their strawberries. With that in mind, it's no wonder a Finnish saying that describes home as sweeter than any foreign place is inspired by those delectable strawberries.

Bite into the sour apple

NORWEGIAN

Bite i det sure eplet

As Snow White will attest, biting into apples is not always associated with positive results. Yet in Scandinavia, biting into a sour apple is the first step towards getting a task done. Similar to the British expression 'biting the bullet', it means that you have to deal with an unpleasant situation. In Denmark, sour apples aren't the worst thing you might face, as there they also have to swallow camels (*sluge en kamel*).

Caught with his beard in the letterbox

SWEDISH

Fastna med skägget i brevlådan

The ultimate nuisance, if you are male, must surely be to trap your beard in a snappy letterbox, especially when said beard has been carefully trimmed, combed and oiled to maintain the highest Scandinavian hipster standards.

The act of getting your beard caught in the letterbox is highly embarrassing, even more so because it is usually self-inflicted. It is roughly equivalent to being 'caught with your hand in the cookie jar' (caught in the act of stealing or defrauding someone) or 'caught with your pants down' (caught in a compromising position). In short, keep your beard out of other people's letterboxes.

Promise gold
and green forests

DANISH

At love guld og grønne skove

While many might promise the moon and the
stars, the modest Scandinavians have gone for the
more down-to-earth, achievable pledge of gold and
green forests. The expression originally comes from
southern Europe, where it is 'to promise mountains
of gold', but since Denmark almost completely
lacks mountains (the highest point in Denmark
is roughly akin to standing on a chair), they have
altered the expression to suit their flatlands and love
of the woods.

Owls in the bog

DANISH

Ugler i mosen

Throughout human history, owls have been
symbols of spirituality, wisdom and intelligence.
They feature in Egyptian hieroglyphs and Greek
myths (owls are especially associated with Athena,
the Greek goddess of wisdom). So, you may wonder,
how on earth did our feathered friends end up in
a Danish bog? 'Owls in the bog' means that there
is something suspicious going on. Originally the
saying was *ulver i mosen* (wolves in the bog –
an equally unlikely scenario), then *ulver* morphed
into *uller* (wool), which sounds very similar to *ugler*
(owls), and that's the way it has remained. Poor
old owls.

Rye in one's wrist

FINNISH

Ruista ranteessa

Popeye happily munched spinach to gain super-strength and the sturdy Scotsman cannot get enough of his porridge oats, but Finns know that physical power comes from having rye in one's wrist. There is a similar expression in Swedish – *råg i ryggen*, which means 'rye in the back'. Choosing dark, brick-like bread over fluffy, buttery brioche guarantees strength and success every time.

I have a hen to pluck with you

NORWEGIAN

Jeg har en høne å plukke med deg

If you borrow your Norwegian friend's car and
don't fill it with petrol afterwards, you can expect
your friend to say that they have a hen to pluck with
you next time you meet. Confused? The expression
is used very much in the same way as the British
'I have a bone to pick with you'.

Have a shit in the blue cupboard

SWEDISH

Skita i det blå skåpet

Pooping in any kind of cupboard might seem like
an odd thing to do, but in 19th-century Sweden
defecating in a red cupboard was *de rigueur*.
Commoners stored their chamber pots in cupboards
painted red, since this was the cheapest paint colour.
Blue, on the other hand, was an expensive hue,
used only for the finest furniture, and particularly
for cupboards containing porcelain and table linen.
Imagine the embarrassment a drunken Swede
might bring upon himself by staggering away
from the dinner table and doing his business in the
wrong cupboard. These days the expression is used
when someone has made a fool of himself or done
something he should not have done.

Even small pots have ears

SWEDISH

Även små grytor har öron

In the English language 'walls have ears' – imagine the secrets they could reveal. In Sweden small pots really do have ears – the handles on cooking pots are known as 'ears' – so they know all about the burnt meatballs, overproved cinnamon buns and close encounters in saunas.

This phrase is used by adults to warn each other that children are in the vicinity and should not be allowed to overhear the conversation ('not in front of the children!').

A delicious herring

DANISH

En lækker sild

Picture the scene: a table at a romantic restaurant –
an eager young chap proffers a diamond ring to his
beloved, and proposes. The lady beams and accepts,
her hand thrust out. Overjoyed, he slips the ring
onto her finger: 'You have made me the happiest
man alive, you delicious herring…' To be likened
to a fish wouldn't usually be regarded as much of
a compliment, but in Scandinavia, and Denmark
specifically, herrings are thought of very highly.
Calling the object of your desire 'a delicious herring'
is one of the highest compliments you can bestow.

The sauna of learning

FINNISH

Opin sauna

You can learn a lot by going to university, but
nothing sets you up for life like a qualification from
The School of Hard Knocks. Or, as the Finns call
it, *opin sauna*, 'the sauna of learning'. Much time is
spent in the sauna in Finland: it is estimated that
there are between 2 and 3 million saunas to cater
for its population of just over 5 million people. So it
truly is where you learn the essential lessons of life.

You should not judge the dog on its hair

NORWEGIAN

Man skal ikke skue hunden på hårene

There are many sensible ways to judge a dog – by its musculature and gait, the cleanliness and sharpness of its teeth, and by how its tail arches. Judging a dog on its hair proves only one thing – that you are shallow and vain. If you are to prosper in life, you should avoid judging a book by its cover and a dog by its hair.

Clear as sausage broth

SWEDISH

Klart som korvspad

Try boiling a sausage in water and you'll quickly
figure out that the resulting broth is anything but
clear. In contrast to the British expression 'clear
as mud', which it resembles most, this Swedish
phrase counterintuitively refers to something that
is obvious – not the other way round. It's somewhat
bewildering, and in this instance one has to
attribute the usage to the Swedish sense of humour,
characterised by large doses of irony and sarcasm.

Like the cat around hot porridge

SWEDISH

Gå som katten kring het gröt

Goldilocks tasted her way through three bowls of porridge before she found the one that was 'just right'; like her, Swedish cats hesitate and pad around a bowl of hot, steaming oatmeal for as long as possible, in the hope that it will cool down.

The meaning of the phrase is similar to 'beating around the bush' – i.e. that someone is procrastinating or deliberately avoiding a difficult situation.

Have clean flour in the bag

DANISH

Have rent mel i posen

In the 19th century, long before anyone worried about white carbs, only millers who sold pure flour were considered trustworthy. Many millers experimented with mixing wheat flour with ground bark from birch, pine, elder and lime trees to eke out the flour they sold at the markets. Customers would ask the vendor if he had 'clean flour in the bag', and judge their trustworthiness accordingly.

Today the expression is used to describe someone who has nothing to hide or has a clean conscience, and is similar to the British expression 'to have a clean sheet'.

Let me show you where a chicken pees from

FINNISH

Näytän sulle, mistä kana pissii

Never mind the old question about the chicken and the egg, if a Finnish person offers to show you where a chicken pees from, they are simply saying 'let me show you how it's done'. Come to think of it, where *does* a chicken pee from…?

Talk straight from the liver

NORWEGIAN

Snakke rett fra levra

Have you ever come across a straight-talking Scandinavian? The chances are pretty high that you have, and if they happen to be Norwegian, they may have 'talked straight from the liver'. This expression, which means that someone speaks frankly and says exactly what she thinks, is from a time when people thought that the liver was the body's centre of feelings and emotions.

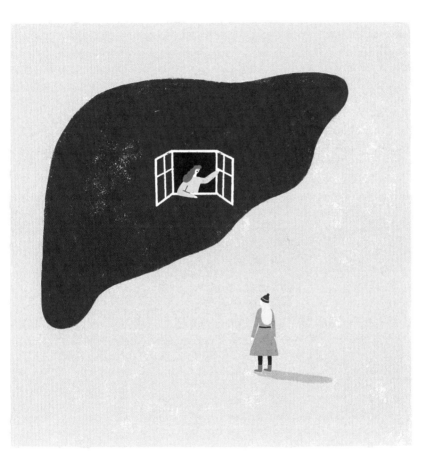

Put rhubarb on...

SWEDISH

Lägga rabarber på

The Swedes don't put towels on sun-loungers ridiculously early in the morning to secure the best spots by the hotel pool. Instead, they will 'put rhubarb' on something they want to claim as their own.

The Swedish for rhubarb is *rabarber*, which sounds very similar to the word *embargo*, and as this was a borrowed and unusual term for the Swedes, it is thought that the saying comes from a mix-up of these two words. Makes perfect sense, right? Now, let me put rhubarb on that news story…

Hot on the porridge

SWEDISH

Vara het på gröten

Hold your horses! Step away from that delicious breakfast. Don't ask me where the Scandinavian obsession with porridge comes from (see pages 39 and 63), but someone who's a little too keen and impatient is described as being 'hot on the porridge' in Swedish, or 'wild in the warmth' (*vild i varmen*) in Danish. Also similar to 'look before you leap', in that you might want to check the temperature of your porridge before tucking in and burning your tongue.

Just pat the horse

DANISH

Klap lige hesten

When a Danish person is worked up and needs to
calm down, don't tell her to take a chill pill; instead
tell her 'just pat the horse'. She will understand
what you mean, even if there is no horse in sight.
This presumably refers to the therapeutic nature
of petting an animal, though snuggling a puppy or
stroking a cat might be a more practical alternative.

Even the crow sings with its own voice

FINNISH

Äänellänsä se variskin laulaa

Crows are not known for being beautiful singers, but at least with these sinister-looking birds, what you hear is very much what you get. Their loud, harsh caws are expressed earnestly and without embellishment. This saying is an encouragement that we should not feel ashamed of a lack of talent or bad performance – that it's okay to try your best and be yourself. Tell that to Simon Cowell.

Float on the (pork) fat

NORWEGIAN

Flyte på flesket

Can there be any more obvious sign that the
Romans never extended their imperial reach to
Scandinavia? While the rest of Europe, south
of the Baltic Sea, might rest on their laurels, the
Norwegians float on the pork fat. This means that
someone is relying too much on their reputation and
tends to sit around complacently instead of working.

Write like a crow

SWEDISH

Skriva som en kråka

Edgar Allan Poe's raven may have 'quoth',
but thank heavens he didn't write, because his
handwriting would have been illegible. So goes the
saying 'to write like a crow', which means 'to write
messily'. A sprawling signature is often referred to
as 'crow feet' (*kråkfötter*).

It's blowing half a pelican

DANISH

Det blæser en halv pelikan

Commonly uttered when it is really windy, 'it's blowing half a pelican' may derive from the fact that *pelikan* rhymes (sort of) with *orkan* (hurricane). On the Beaufort scale half a pelican translates as a solid 11 (which would make a *whole* pelican an inconceivable 22), whereas a herring gull would rank a 7 (moderate gale), and a blue tit a meagre 2 (light breeze).

Not all the Moomins are in the valley

FINNISH
Ei ole kaikki muumit laaksossa

Where might the Moomins be, if not in the valley? Perhaps Moomintroll has decided to go on a midnight adventure with Snufkin, making Moominmamma sick with worry?

Tove Jansson's beloved children's characters are essential Finnish cultural and design icons, so a distinct lack of Moomins would ring alarm bells. Perhaps that's why they have become part of this expression that means the same as 'the lights are on, but nobody's home'.

In the middle of the butter eye

NORWEGIAN

Å være midt i smørøyet

To find yourself in the middle of the butter eye is to be in the sweetest spot of them all! Families used to eat porridge from a big communal bowl, where a blob of butter was put in the middle. As they ate their way towards the centre of the bowl, the person who reached the pool of melted butter first had hit the jackpot, hence the expression.

Make a hen out of a feather

SWEDISH

Göra en höna av en fjäder

Hans Christian Andersen wasn't one to shy away from teaching kiddywinks a lesson or two about morals. In his fairytale *It's Quite True!* he wrote about the power of exaggeration, and how a rumour can change and expand out of all proportion, the more it is retold. This story is the root of the Swedish saying 'make a hen out of a feather', which sits somewhere between the two British idioms 'a storm in a teacup' and 'a mountain out of a molehill'. In Norwegian the saying is 'make a feather into five hens' (*gjøre en fjær til fem høns*) and in Danish it is 'a feather can easily turn into five hens' (*en fjer kan let blive til fem høns*).

There is a dog buried here

SWEDISH

Här ligger en hund begraven

The origins of this expression are unknown,
but what is certain is that it means the same as
'something fishy is going on'. So perhaps something
very suspicious has sparked these animal-based
Swedish idioms? Author Stephen King would
no doubt be fascinated to know that one of the
oldest pet cemeteries ('sematarys'?) was founded
in Stockholm in 1840, and the horse from Ingmar
Bergman's classic movie *The Seventh Seal* is buried
there. Fun times.

It's raining cobbler boys

Det regner skomagerdrenge

When the rain is hammering down in Denmark, it is cobbler boys who are said to be falling from the sky. Presumably with hammers, nails and a few anvils for good measure. Animal-loving Brits prefer to be drenched with cats and dogs, and you might want to give rainstorms in France a miss, where it often rains 'like a pissing cow'.

Whoever reaches for the spruce, falls down onto the juniper

FINNISH

Ken kuuseen kurkottaa, se katajaan kapsahtaa

In some corners of the world, the juniper's status is elevated above that of all other plants. That's because it is a vital ingredient in that most British of liquors, gin. In Scandinavia, however, where spruce-tip syrup made from the first shoots that appear every spring is a delicacy, the tables are turned. Hence this pessimistic Finnish warning.

Paint the devil
on the wall

NORWEGIAN

Male fanden på veggen

Scandinavians are known for painting all their walls white, although one or two of the boldest may go for a daring light grey shade, or a raunchy eggshell colour. So who on earth paints the devil on the wall? The saying dates back to the 17th century, when it was believed that something terrible would happen or an accident might occur simply by talking about it. Nowadays, it is used when someone portrays something as much worse than it is.

Put onion on the salmon

SWEDISH

Lägga lök på laxen

Few things are dearer to a Swede than a plate of fish. Pickled herring, poached cod, smoked and cured salmon – you name it. However, you can perhaps have too much of a good thing, as the Swedes demonstrate with this saying, which has evolved to mean that you might be making something even worse. So whatever you do, don't put onion on that salmon.

Step into the spinach

DANISH

Træde i spinaten

While traditional winemakers use the old and
trusted method of foot stomping for crushing the
grapes, the Scandinavians only step into things
when they unintentionally cause embarrassment or
act in a tactless way. Danes step into the spinach, the
Norwegians step in the salad (*tråkke i salaten*) and
the Swedes in the piano (*trampa i klaveret*). These
expressions all correspond to the British saying 'put
one's foot in it'.

Throw the spoon into the corner

FINNISH

Heittää lusikka nurkkaan

If you ever get invited to a Finnish dinner party, be very, very careful how you handle the cutlery. Whatever you do, do not throw your spoon into the corner. Unless, that is, you have had enough of life, as this expression has the same meaning as 'bite the dust' and 'kick the bucket'.

Born behind a brown cheese

NORWEGIAN

Å være født bak en brunost

There are many curious places where one might be born, but the one that takes the prize must surely be behind a brown cheese. *Brunost*, the Norwegian cheese in question, has become a national treasure. It is highly regarded by its countrymen, so it is rather puzzling that it is considered an insult to suggest that someone was born behind one – implying that the person in question is not particularly bright.

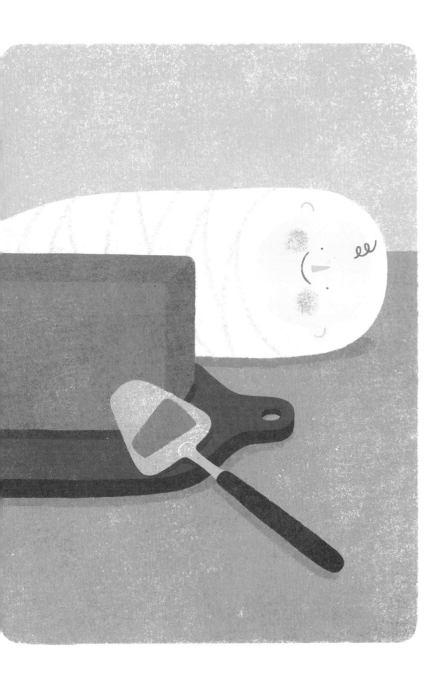

Talk in the beard

SWEDISH

Prata i skägget

Scandinavian beards can't seem to stay out of
trouble. When they're not busy getting stuck in
letterboxes (*Fastna med skägget i brevlådan*, see page
16), they are responsible for all sorts of crimes.
When someone mumbles or speaks unclearly
they are encouraged to stop talking in the beard,
regardless of whether the guilty party even sports
a beard…

Out cycling

DANISH

Ude og cykle

In Copenhagen there are more than half a million bicycle owners. Were everyone to be 'out cycling' on the streets at once, it would be utter chaos. 'Out cycling' therefore suggests someone is completely bonkers. One can only guess how many thousands of people survive the morning commute through sheer luck alone.

Don't have a mouth of birch bark

FINNISH

Ei ole suu tuohesta

If you ask a Finnish person whether they would care for a drink, and they respond by telling you that they do not have a mouth of birch bark, do not fret! They are not being rude – in Finnish this is a perfectly reasonable answer and in fact means that they are an enthusiastic drinker. So, go on and wet your whistle!

A fox behind the ear

NORWEGIAN

En rev bak øret

Foxes generally don't have the greatest of
reputations, often characterised in folklore
and children's literature as being sly and
untrustworthy. It should therefore be no big
surprise that a person who has a fox behind
his ear is keeping something to himself. The
expression has its origins in the Middle Ages,
when many believed that people whose ears
stuck out were suspicious and not to be trusted.

Get paid for old cheese

SWEDISH

Få betalt för gammal ost

Gammalost is a type of traditional cheese that has been made in northern Sweden and Norway since the Viking era; the name literally translates as 'old cheese'. It tastes sharp and pungent, and is not to everyone's liking. To get money for old cheese means that you will be on the receiving end of revenge.

Drag cod to shore

DANISH

Trække torsk i land

Before you start complaining about your other half snoring like a chainsaw, just remember that the Danes have it far worse. There, the sleeping beauties' rumblings bring to mind the repellent sound of cod being pulled ashore, with fins, tails and all scraping over the shingle like a badly played cello. One can only hope that the fish are already dead, otherwise you could add 'immense amount of flapping around' to the list of woes for the poor snorer's partner.

With one's mittens straight

FINNISH

Tumput suorina

Picture Mikko, the Finn, standing in a forest clearing, chopping wood, huffing and puffing, sweat dripping. Now picture his friend, Pekka, also standing in the clearing, but casually relaxed, mittens straight, doing nothing at all. This saying implies that you're not pulling your weight while others are working hard, and must surely come from the fact that very little work can be carried out with mittened hands.

It's completely
on the snout

NORWEGIAN

Det er helt på trynet

As you will have gathered from this book, there
are as many things that unite the Scandinavian
countries as divide them, and here is another prime
example of the latter. Danes take their pigs very
seriously and Denmark is a land known for its fine
bacon. The Norwegians, however, refer to the pig
when they wish to create a surreal image, or convey
that an idea is utterly ridiculous.

Slide in on a shrimp sandwich/banana skin

SWEDISH

Halka in på en räkmacka / ett bananskal

Slipping on a banana peel is a well-known staple of slapstick comedy, but in Sweden its meaning is entirely different. To slide in on a banana skin or, even better, a shrimp sandwich, is considered a stroke of luck, meaning that someone has attained a privileged position in life easily but perhaps without deserving it.

Live on a big foot

DANISH

Leve på en stor fod

Next time your mum gasps at Lady Gaga's choice of footwear, and remarks that everything was better in the good old days, you can remind her about the fashions of the Middle Ages. Both men and women wore shoes with extremely long, pointed toes. There were laws in place to dictate the length of the shoe: the longer the shoe, the higher the social class of the person sporting them. The nobility were permitted two-foot lengths, merchants one-foot length and peasants, a mere half. To 'live on a big foot' means that one is flaunting newly acquired wealth, and has a lifestyle that they cannot really afford ('living beyond one's means').

Comes loose like Grandma's tooth

FINNISH

Irtoaa kuin mummon hammas

The origins of this saying, which means that something goes very, very smoothly, are unknown. Perhaps it comes from a dentist, who was asked to rate how easy it was to pull teeth from various family members?!

Crossing the river to get water

NORWEGIAN

Gå over bekken etter vann

This expression originates from a time when there
was no such luxury as running water. People had
to tackle many obstacles on their way to obtain
fresh water. In Norway the obvious dangers might
include a hungry and recently hibernating bear
lurking behind the village well, or the lake being
frozen solid, so that one had to hack off pieces of
ice with a huge axe before thawing them. Given
all these hazards, the act of crossing the river for
water, rather than dipping one's bucket at the
nearest shore, would have been considered entirely
unnecessary – and, therefore, pretty foolish.
Nowadays the saying is used to refer to solving a
problem in a clumsy, roundabout way when there is
a much easier and more obvious solution.

No cow on the ice

SWEDISH

Ingen ko på isen

Back in the days when the cows of Scandinavia could roam freely all year round, they were routinely taken down to lakes to be watered. In the winter the farmers would make a drinking hole in the frozen lake to allow the parched bovines to slake their thirst. Sometimes, if the ice was too thin to withstand the weight of half a ton of grass-fed beef, the ice would break. There was no need to panic, however: as long as the cow's rump and hind legs were on solid ground, she could be safely encouraged back from the water's edge with a firm tug of the tail. Nowadays the expression is used to calm someone down, when you want them to chill out and not worry.

It costs the whites
of the eyes

DANISH

Det koster det hvide ud af øjnene

If there's no price tag, proceed with caution, as in
all likelihood you won't be able to afford the item
in question. If you make the mistake of enquiring
about the price, you are likely to get an unpleasant
surprise – one that might cause you to widen
your eyes in alarm. Perhaps that's why something
described in English as 'costing an arm and a leg'
costs the whites of the eyes in Danish.

It's only blueberries

NORWEGIAN

Det er bare blåbær

We have already learned that the otherwise modest Scandinavians rate their berries highly (see page 12) and find them nothing short of magic. The long summer days and midnight sun create an abundance of wild, seasonal berries that you probably won't have heard of unless you have visited a certain furniture shop famous for its flatpacks (lingonberries anyone? Cloudberries?). Unlike the oversized shop-bought and pale-fleshed blueberries, Scandinavian blueberries are deep purple all the way through and as packed with flavour as they are with antioxidants (and a mysterious ability to stain clothes forever). It is therefore slightly puzzling how this saying came about, as it means 'something easy', 'insignificant', or 'a small amount of something'.

PUBLISHING DIRECTOR
Sarah Lavelle

ASSISTANT EDITOR
Stacey Cleworth

SENIOR DESIGNER
Emily Lapworth

ILLUSTRATOR
Nastia Sleptsova

PRODUCTION
Nikolaus Ginelli

Published in 2019 by Quadrille,
an imprint of Hardie Grant

Quadrille
52–54 Southwark Street
London SE1 1UN
quadrille.com

Text © Quadrille 2019
Artwork © Nastia Sleptsova 2019
Design and layout © Quadrille 2019

All rights reserved. No part of this book may be
reproduced, stored in a retrieval system or transmitted
in any form or by any means, electronic, electrostatic,
magnetic tape, mechanical, photocopying, recording or
otherwise, without the prior permission in writing of
the publisher.

Cataloguing in Publication Data:
a catalogue record for this book is
available from the British Library.

ISBN 978 1 78713 472 0
Printed in China